WEEKLY **WR** READER®
EARLY LEARNING LIBRARY

Where People **Work**
¿Dónde **trabaja** la gente?

What Happens at a
Bike Shop?

¿Qué pasa en
una tienda de bicicletas?

by/por Kathleen Pohl

Reading consultant/Consultora de lectura: Susan Nations, M.Ed., author, literacy coach,
consultant in literacy development/autora, tutora de alfabetización, consultora de desarrollo de la lectura

Please visit our web site at: www.garethstevens.com
For a free color catalog describing Weekly Reader® Early Learning Library's list
of high-quality books, call 1-877-445-5824 (USA) or 1-800-387-3178 (Canada).
Weekly Reader® Early Learning Library's fax: (414) 336-0164.

Library of Congress Cataloging-in-Publication Data

Pohl, Kathleen.
    What happens at a bike shop? = ¿Qué pasa en una tienda de bicicletas? / Kathleen Pohl.
      p. cm. — (Where people work = ¿Dónde trabaja la gente?)
    Includes bibliographical references and index.
    ISBN-10: 0-8368-7386-6 — ISBN-13: 978-0-8368-7386-3 (lib. bdg.)
    ISBN-10: 0-8368-7393-9 — ISBN-13: 978-0-8368-7393-1 (softcover)
    1. Bicycles—Juvenile literature.   2. Bicycle stores—Juvenile literature.
  I. Title. II. Title: Qué pasa en una tienda de bicletas? III. Series: Pohl, Kathleen. Where people work (Spanish & English).
TL412.P6518   2007a
381'.456292272—dc22
                  2006016796

This edition first published in 2007 by
Weekly Reader® Early Learning Library
A Member of the WRC Media Family of Companies
330 West Olive Street, Suite 100
Milwaukee, Wisconsin 53212 USA

Copyright © 2007 by Weekly Reader® Early Learning Library

Buddy® is a registered trademark of Weekly Reader Corporation. Used under license.

Managing editor: Dorothy L. Gibbs
Art direction: Tammy West
Cover design and page layout: Scott M. Krall
Picture research: Diane Laska-Swanke and Kathleen Pohl
Photographer: Jack Long
Translation: Tatiana Acosta and Guillermo Gutiérrez

Acknowledgments: The publisher thanks Dominique and Sigrunn Mosley and John Jensen
for modeling in this book. Special thanks to John Jensen, of Johnson's Cycle & Fitness, for
his expert consulting and the use of his shop's facilities.

Printed in the United States of America

1 2 3 4 5 6 7 8 9 10 09 08 07 06

Hi, Kids!

I'm Buddy, your Weekly Reader® pal. Have you ever visited a bike shop? I'm here to show and tell what happens at a bike shop. So, come on. Turn the page and read along!

– – – – – – – –

¡Hola, chicos!

Soy Buddy, su amigo de Weekly Reader®. ¿Han estado alguna vez en una tienda de bicicletas? Estoy aquí para contarles lo que pasa en una tienda de bicicletas. Así que vengan conmigo. ¡Pasen la página y vamos a leer!

Dominic wants to buy a bike. This bike shop has lots of them, in all sizes and colors!

– – – – – – – –

Dominic quiere comprar una bicicleta. ¡En esta tienda hay un montón de bicicletas, de todos los tamaños y colores!

Some bikes are red. Some are
blue. Some have three wheels.
Some have two.

— — — — — — — —

Algunas bicicletas son rojas.
Otras son azules. Algunas tienen
tres ruedas. Otras tienen dos.

Mr. Jensen owns the bike shop.
He is helping Dominic choose a
bike. Dominic's new bike must
be just the right size for him.

— — — — — — — —

El señor Jensen es el dueño de la
tienda. Está ayudando a Dominic a
elegir una bicicleta. La bicicleta de
Dominic tiene que ser del tamaño justo.

He can try out some bikes right in
Mr. Jensen's shop. Whee! Look
out, Dominic!

— — — — — — — —

Dominic puede probar algunas
bicicletas dentro de la tienda del señor
Jensen. ¡Uau! ¡Con cuidado, Dominic!

Mr. Jensen has a workshop in the back of his store. He has lots of tools in his workshop. He uses the tools to fix broken bikes.

— — — — — — — — —

El señor Jensen tiene un taller en la parte trasera de la tienda. En el taller hay muchas herramientas. Las usa para reparar las bicicletas estropeadas.

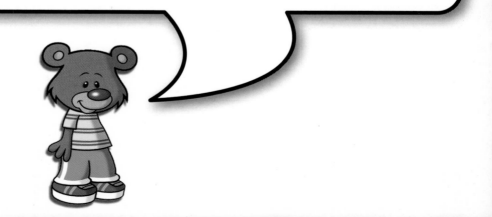

Mr. Jensen also uses his tools on new bikes. New bikes come in pieces. The pieces are packed in boxes.

– – – – – – – – –

El señor Jensen también usa las herramientas con las bicicletas nuevas. Las bicicletas nuevas vienen desarmadas. Las piezas están en cajas.

Mr. Jensen uses tools to put the pieces together. First, he attaches the front wheel. He uses a tool called a **wrench**.

— — — — — — — —

El señor Jensen usa herramientas para unir las piezas. Primero, pone la rueda delantera. Usa una herramienta llamada **llave inglesa**.

wrench/
llave inglesa

17

Next, Mr. Jensen attaches the **pedals**. Then he will attach the seat and the **handlebars**.

— — — — — — — —

Después, el señor Jensen pone los **pedales**. Más adelante, pondrá el asiento y el **manillar**.

pedal/pedal

Dominic's bike is ready to ride. Don't forget to wear a safety helmet, Dominic!

– – – – – – – –

La bicicleta de Dominic está lista. ¡No te olvides de ponerte el casco, Dominic!

 # Glossary/Glosario

handlebars — the bar across the front of a bike that has a handle at each end for steering

helmet — a hard hat that keeps the head safe

pedals — the parts of a bike moved by the feet to make the bike go forward

workshop — a place with tools where a person can build or fix things

wrench — a tool used to twist something to make it tight

— — — — — — — —

casco — pieza dura que sirve para proteger la cabeza

llave inglesa — herramienta que se usa para hacer girar algo y apretarlo

manillar — barra en la parte delantera de la bicicleta, con un mango en cada extremo, y que se usa para cambiar de dirección

pedales — partes que, al ser empujadas con los pies, hacen que avance la bicicleta

taller — lugar con herramientas donde una persona puede hacer o reparar cosas

 # For More Information/Más información

Books/Libros

Bicicletas. Lee y aprende (series). Lola M. Schaefer (Heinemann Library)

En bicicleta. Seguridad (series). Kyle Carter (Rourke)

How Is a Bicycle Made? Angela Royston (Heinemann Library)

I Can Ride a Bike. Edana Eckart (Childrens Press)

Look Out! A Story about Safety on Bicycles. The Hero Club (series). Cindy Leaney (Rourke)

Index/Índice

bikes 4, 6, 8, 10, 12, 14, 20
buying 4
colors 4, 6
handlebars 18

helmet 20
pedals 18
safety 20
seat 18
sizes 4, 8

tools 12, 14, 16
wheels 6, 16
workshop 12
wrench 16

- -

asiento 18
bicicletas 4, 6, 8, 10, 12, 14, 20
casco 20
colores 4, 6

comprar 4
herramientas 12, 14, 16
llave inglesa 16
manillar 18
pedales 18

ruedas 6, 16
taller 12
tamaños 4, 8

About the Author

Kathleen Pohl has written and edited many children's books. Among them are animal tales, rhyming books, retold classics, and the forty-book series *Nature Close-Ups*. She also served for many years as top editor of *Taste of Home* and *Country Woman* magazines. She and her husband, Bruce, live among beautiful Wisconsin woods and share their home with six goats, a llama, and all kinds of wonderful woodland creatures.

- -

Información sobre la autora

Kathleen Pohl ha escrito y corregido muchos libros infantiles. Entre ellos hay cuentos de animales, libros de rimas, versiones nuevas de cuentos clásicos y la serie de cuarenta libros *Nature Close-Ups*. Además, trabajó durante muchos años como directora de las revistas *Taste of Home* y *Country Woman*. Kathleen vive con su marido, Bruce, en los bellos bosques de Wisconsin. Ambos comparten su hogar con seis cabras, una llama y todo tipo de maravillosos animales del bosque.